On Kruger Pond:

Charlie's Story

By Gerry Kruger

Illustrated by: Janice Hawkins
Edited by: Ginny Kanter

To Fred, who loved Charlie and often requested that I record his adventures by writing a book, and to Rob, who stood by me and encouraged me throughout my endeavors.

Acknowledgments

I am deeply indebted to my writing group, whose steadfast support and invaluable critiques made this book possible: Peggy Brown, Sharon Davie, Marian Morgan, Susan Guerrant, Linn Harrison, Bruce Hillman, and Sharon Hostler. A special thanks to Susan Guerrant, who suggested that I read my essays on WVTF.

WVTF's airing the essays and the listeners who contacted me to show their appreciation of them were instrumental in my decision to publish this book.

Janice Hawkins, my illustrator and mentor, guided me thoughtfully and patiently throughout the publishing process and introduced me to a top-notch editor, Ginny Kanter.

Contents

Kruger Pond

In the seventies, looking at property in Albemarle County became a regular weekend pastime for my husband Fred and me. I was satisfied with our life in Chesterfield County, but Fred yearned for views of the Blue Ridge Mountains and wanted to be close to his alma mater, the University of Virginia, so we could make 20-minute trips to football and basketball games instead of driving for hours. That appealed to me too.

Our realtor, a Charlottesville friend, showed us property weekend after weekend. Finally he told us about the perfect lot with mountain views a few miles west of Charlottesville. We were ambling about this property, carefully inspecting every possible house site, when Fred stopped and craned his neck. "What's that?" he asked.

Just below us, almost hidden by heavy brush, trees, and vines was a large pond. An energetic wood duck darted this way and that, disappearing under the water for what seemed to be a dangerously long time and then emerging several yards away.

"What about the land over there?" Fred pointed to the parcel of land surrounding the pond. "Is that property for sale?"

"I'll check, but I don't think you'll have mountain views," replied our friend.

"It doesn't matter. If we can see water birds like that from our house, that's the lot I want."

Within a year we found jobs and moved to Charlottesville. Fred was a data processing manager for a company in Crozet, and I found a job teaching English at Charlottesville High School. As soon as we sold our house in Chesterfield, we began building our home on the pond. At least once a week we visited the property to see how our house was progressing and to see the wood duck or any other waterfowl that happened by. After several months, anticipation turned to disappointment. Not only was there no wood duck—we encountered no wildlife whatsoever during the entire time our house was being constructed. It wasn't until we moved and began keeping the grass trimmed around the pond that Mabel and Max, our first resident Canada geese, arrived.

Fred immediately bought corn for the geese and a pair of binoculars for us. Soon Mabel and Max would swim toward our house the minute they saw our car in the driveway, and if I didn't feed them at once, they followed me until I did. When I bent over to pull a weed and felt something tug at my shorts, it was Mabel reminding me that she and Max were ready for their dinner!

One day I came home from school and saw Max by himself in the pond. He completely ignored me. *What happened to Mabel?* I wondered.

"I don't know what's wrong with the geese," I said to Fred, without giving him my usual kiss as he came through the front door from work.

"What do you mean?" Fred set his folder on the dining room table and faced me.

"Well, Max didn't come to me when I drove in from school, and Mabel is missing."

"Let's see." Fred scooped the binoculars from the nearby shelf and rushed to the deck.

Max was still in the same spot in the pond next to the woods.

"Wait! I think I see her." Fred was focusing the binoculars on the woods next to Max's post. "There she is! She's sitting in the woods. I think she has a nest!"

"Let me see." I reached for the binoculars. "So that's it," I said. "Max is guarding Mabel and the eggs. No wonder he didn't come to me today."

At least once a day Mabel took a break and joined Max for a swim. After much splashing and bathing, both geese waddled to the feeding spot in front of our house and ate the corn I pitched to them.

One day neither goose was in sight when I arrived home from school. I grabbed the binoculars and spotted in the distance a pair of geese walking slowly, one behind the other. Between them were six fuzzy balls that wobbled unsteadily. The entire family made their way up to the driveway where I stood. Max was standing tall and proud as I inspected the new additions. After applauding and congratulating them, I sprinkled some corn in front of the new goslings, and all but one baby goose skittered away. Undaunted, that baby stepped up to me and ate a kernel of corn from my hand.

This goose was not only the first of the goslings to eat from my hand. He was also first in line when Mabel led the family across the pond with Max bringing up the rear, and first to scramble up the muddy bank. He fought off any creature that dared to eat his share of the corn I threw out, and when flying lessons began, he flew faster and farther than any of his brothers and sisters. Little did we know that this alpha male would become both the protector and terror of Kruger Pond. He lived up to the name we gave him—Tony, after Tony Soprano of gangster fame. He instilled fear in every creature that dared to invade his territory.

One day a raggedy, broken-winged, and flightless goose showed up at Kruger Pond. We named him Charlie and did our best to feed him, but he was too intimidated to let us get close enough. Not about to tolerate this lame outcast, Tony dived at Charlie with lightning speed and pecked him ferociously. In fact, Tony's attacks were so vicious that I feared he would kill the interloper. Although he never fought back, Charlie refused to leave.

One morning I witnessed Tony racing across my driveway with Charlie right behind him. How could that be? "Fred," I called, "Charlie's chasing Tony!" All of the geese in front of Charlie were running for their lives into the pond. Then we saw the reason for this mad dash. Behind Charlie was a large black bear, galloping at amazing speed. For a moment we forgot about the geese and marveled at the bear, racing across spring-green grass, his silky fur gleaming in the sunlight of a cloudless sky.

From this moment our parcel of land was transformed into a magical place. There was the satisfying, if brief, illusion of Charlie's dominance over his tormentor, and the realization that Kruger Pond was indeed home to the wildlife we had dreamed of.

Charlie's Here to Stay

The first time I laid eyes on Charlie, he was a broken-down jalopy of a goose. His broken wing stuck out as he limped about, trying to avoid the geese who dove and pecked at him. That raggedy old wing was a signal that he was fair game for ill treatment.

The Kruger Pond bullies made his life miserable if he tried to eat the corn I threw out. In spite of the negative attention he received, Charlie stayed with the flock. It was better than no attention at all. But Charlie's motor wasn't about to sputter and die. No, sir! Little by little, he grew to trust me and allowed me to feed him when no other geese were around. Little by little, he grew stronger and more confident. Little by little, his broken wing became his badge of courage.

No matter how despicable the other geese were, none compared to Tony the Terrible. One day I noticed a commotion in the bushes on the bank near my house. Toting a canoe paddle, I edged up toward the suspicious area to inspect. What did I find inside the shrubs but Tony on top of Charlie, pinning him down, and pecking away. "Tony, stop it!" I hollered. But he kept right on. That's when I shoved the canoe paddle between them and lifted Tony as hard as I could. Tony finally left the scene of the crime and flew away, but poor old Charlie lay dead still. I dialed Fred's work number, but got his voice mail. Beginning to cry, I raced to my neighbor Leon's house and knocked on the door. "Tony's killed Charlie," I sobbed.

"Wait, I'll come with you."

Leon and I went back to the bushes. I thought he'd help me bury Charlie. But, hallelujah, the tomb was empty! Charlie was gone! We looked a few feet away and there was Charlie, limping and peaked, but very much alive.

I'm not sure when I realized that Charlie was here to stay. Perhaps my saving him from Tony's vicious attack cemented our relationship. Canada geese migrate because of food supply, not because of cold weather. They are well equipped to handle the cold, as we who live in Albemarle County know. Albemarle has a large population of Canada geese that stay here year round. Even though I made sure that Charlie had food and water, his inability to fly to different areas to look for food was unquestionably another reason he stayed at my pond throughout the winter.

Nothing bothered Charlie more than not being able to fly. At the end of each summer, all of the geese molted, grew back new feathers, and learned to fly anew. From the top of the hill, they honked, flapped their wings, and took off together toward the pond. It was a thrilling sight. They flew as far as they could and fell into the water if they weren't strong enough to stay airborne. Once they could fly the entire length of the pond, they left for the winter. Well, the first summer he was here, Charlie must have run down that hill fifty times, honking and flapping his wings, but his broken wing kept him from lifting. The day the other geese left him behind, Charlie honked incessantly. Week after week he just looked up at the empty sky and honked.

Charlie stayed with us every winter after the other geese left for greener pastures. I made sure he was fed in bad weather. Dr. Kelly at the Wildlife Center, a rehabilitation center just across the Blue Ridge Mountains from Albemarle County, said to add some greens to his water when the ground froze. Whenever there was a period of frigid weather, I waited for him to appear at his feeding spot and placed a pan of cut-up kale and water beside his corn.

If I went away for a day or two, Charlie would give me an unforgiving stare when I returned. Naturally I would think he wanted me to feed him. "Okay, Charlie," I'd say. "I know you want your corn." I'd pour some next to him, and he would just keep on staring at me, ignoring it. "I'm sorry I wasn't here for you, Charlie. Were you lonesome without me?" After listening to me apologize for a few more minutes, he'd turn away and eat his corn.

Charlie's Quest

I wasn't sure about Charlie's intentions when it came to females. I had been the only woman in his life until 2001, and for a while I thought he was a confirmed bachelor. In time, I learned that he wasn't a bachelor by choice. Charlie struggled and floundered, but he never gave up trying to attract a female.

"Do you have any female geese that can't fly?" Fred asked Dr. Kelly at the Wildlife Center in Waynesboro. Poor Charlie had grown so desperate for female companionship by the spring of 2001 that he was making advances toward the mates of the other geese on our pond. Being unable to fly didn't keep him from having frequent bouts with jealous ganders. Fred was not one to sit idly by and let poor Charlie pine away. As he hung up the phone, his triumphant grin was a dead giveaway that he had found the perfect match for Charlie.

The Wildlife Center offered Honey. She had a birth defect that caused her to fall every time she took a step, but she was so tame that she would let us hold her in our laps. We quickly fell in love with her. The first time she laid eyes on Charlie, she fell in love with him. She followed him everywhere, slipping and falling and often getting stuck in the mud at the water's edge.

One morning I saw Charlie standing behind my car, blocking me in. I blew the horn and backed up a little, expecting him to move as he usually did, but he wouldn't budge. I scanned the pond and saw Honey, mired in the mud. She couldn't get out, and Charlie wasn't about to let me out either—at least not until I did something about Honey. Fred was a city boy and had never set foot in our pond. Ill-equipped for this particular mission, he donned an old bathing suit and rescued Honey in the November cold. She flapped her wings and sprayed him with mud from head to toe. Because she had no way of escaping predators, and Fred was taking three showers a day due to the frequent rescue missions, we finally made the heartbreaking decision to take her back.

When Beauty showed up the following year, Charlie was smitten mightily. She was dainty and sleek with the elegance of Audrey Hepburn. Much to my delight, Beauty liked me, too. She affectionately drew close to me, stared at my red-painted toenails, and gave them tender pecks. If Beauty strayed from his side, Charlie bobbed his head at her ferociously. They spent every day together, and we thought Charlie had found his mate at last.

The problem was the nights. As soon as dusk set in, Beauty would fly away and leave poor Charlie honking mournfully. At first he tried to follow her. The sight of him hurrying after her on foot would have been hilarious had his poor heart not been broken. The next day Beauty would return and get the full head-bobbing treatment. After he scolded her vociferously, they would settle down until she deserted him once more. This lasted for most of the summer until Beauty left for good.

Fred and I refused to give up on Charlie's quest to find a mate. Charlie was so determined to have a female in his life that we knew he would eventually accomplish his mission. After all, his survival in the wild without being able to fly was just as miraculous as getting a female goose to remain grounded in order to be with him.

The Locked Door

Fred once took a picture of me smiling proudly as I displayed the tiniest non-cherry tomato known to exist. Although the tomato is my vegetable of choice, I have never mastered the art of cultivating anything like those that the other teachers used to bring to school. They complained about being overrun with mountains of plump, juicy tomatoes. I envied their dilemma. I planted five or six tomato plants and was lucky to have five or six tomatoes before the worms or deer ate the rest.

"I think I'll plant the tomatoes today," I thought aloud to Fred as we ate breakfast. I had just finished preparing final exams, marking the end of another year of teaching. It was the Saturday before Memorial Day in 2002, and both of us looked forward to a long weekend.

"Maybe I'll cut back some of the brush and tree branches," Fred responded. "I'd like to make an escape route for Charlie."

Fred and I were concerned about Tony's increased aggressiveness toward Charlie. It had always been obvious that Tony didn't want this lame goose at our pond, but his attacks had become more vicious. Tony had begun to take off from one side of the pond and dive at his arch rival with such force that I wondered how long Charlie could dodge such a bullet. Unable to fly, Charlie was no match for Tony in an open area, but on a path through the woods, he could easily win a foot race, having had so much practice.

I cared about Charlie, but my feelings couldn't compare to Fred's. Fred took everything to the next level, and whatever he did was executed with gusto. He told me that when he first learned to write, he tore holes in the paper erasing errors. He wanted to be certain that his mistakes were completely obliterated.

The ritual he followed when merely locking a door took incredibly long. He pulled on the knob again and again before he was convinced that it was truly locked. Once he called to say he would be home late because he had pulled off the doorknob to his office and couldn't leave until a locksmith came to repair it.

I started to dig in the backyard. Nearby, Fred finished cutting dead tree branches and was clearing Charlie's path through the woods. The sun was broiling hot, and Fred was drenched in perspiration.

"Don't overdo it," I warned. "Let me bring you some water."

"No, thanks," he said and continued to hack away at the weeds with grim determination.

I ignored his response and went into the house to get the water only to hear the phone ring. It was a parent calling about her son. While I was speaking to her, Fred came to the door and called my name. I opened the door and knew he was in trouble. All the color had drained from his face, and he struggled to make it to a chair. I asked him if I should call 911. He nodded, "Yes."

When the rescue squad arrived, they examined him and informed me they were taking him to the hospital. I decided to follow rather than ride with him, so I could bring him back home if he didn't need to stay.

As they carried him out, he looked at me and said, "Don't forget to lock the door." That was my Fred, always worried that I wouldn't be as thorough as he was. I arrived at the hospital to learn that Fred had died of a massive heart attack and there was nothing more the doctors could do. I remember thinking I would wake up from this bad dream and find him beside me.

A week later, I was back at school, working with one of my students who had stayed late to get extra help. She quietly asked what his last words to me were. I replied, "Don't forget to lock the door."

She said, "He was more concerned about you than himself."

"Yes," I said.

A patio now covers the area where I planted the tomatoes on the day he died. I couldn't bring myself to plant anything there again. The path Fred cleared through the woods remains to this day.

Triumph!

In October 2006, Madame, a haughty and distrustful female goose, landed on Kruger Pond and hissed whenever I came near her. She was no Beauty and I wondered what Charlie saw in her, but soon it became evident that Charlie and Madame were a couple. Her most distinctive features were white eyebrows that made her look as if she disapproved of me. *He's on the rebound,* I thought. *She'll be history as soon as the first frost comes. That's when she'll find out he can't fly.* But what do I know? Madame gave up flying and stayed with Charlie throughout the winter.

It was during the spring of 2007 that I noticed Charlie had been alone for several days. *Oh, no. Charlie's lost another one,* I thought. When I threw him some corn, he ignored it and stepped closer to me than ever before. "What's the matter, Charlie?" I asked. He fixed his eyes hard on mine as if he wanted to tell me something.

I began to look around the property and noticed a goose perched on the dam. Could it be Madame on a nest? Carefully I made my way through tangled vines and thorny blackberry stems from the previous summer. There, on a nest, was a goose with white eyebrows! She sprang three feet in the air when I placed a handful of corn next to her. Suddenly I could see five lovely snow-white eggs in a perfectly constructed nest that looked as cozy as a warm blanket. Charlie was instantly at her side, giving me a you-should-know-better look.

"OK, Charlie. I'm sorry. I won't get close to her or her precious eggs again," I apologized. He seemed to shrug his broken wing and went back to his guard post in the water.

It was then that I realized I had misjudged as haughtiness Madame's shyness and sense of responsibility. Madame was no flirt looking for a fling. She had an important mission and needed to be cautious around strangers like me. I had to admire her loyalty to Charlie and realized I didn't mind being the other woman in his life.

Canada goose eggs usually hatch within 25 to 30 days, so I counted the days and watched the nest, thinking how excited Fred would have been to share this with me. Meanwhile Charlie bravely guarded the nest against the drooling dogs, slithering black snakes, sharp-eyed hawks, and hungry red foxes lurking about. After more than 30 days, my heart sank. Madame's droopy eyes and worn feathers revealed her fatigue from sitting on the nest so long. Her eggs, once clean and white, looked dingy and drab.

One morning I heard some unusually loud honking and splashing. Charlie was standing near the nest instead of guarding from his usual spot in the pond. *Could this be it?* I wondered. *Is Charlie actually going to be a dad?* When I returned from school that afternoon, there was an empty, deserted nest and no sign of Charlie or Madame. Then I spotted Charlie climbing over a stone wall on the hill beside my house, and behind him, Madame. *At least he still has her,* I thought. *Perhaps they'll try again and build a nest in a better place. But wait ... could it be?* A newly hatched gosling was scrambling over the wall behind them. It was difficult to believe that a one-day-old gosling could climb a stone wall with such agility and ease. "Charlie, I should have known you'd father an athlete," I said.

I was sorry to have missed the moment Charlie Junior hatched, but I think Fred was watching.

Junior Gets It

"Honkk! ...Honkk! ...Honkk!" I was accustomed to Charlie's distinctive call. That high pitch at the end of his honk always made him sound more desperate than the other Canada geese at our pond, perhaps because he *was* desperate. No matter how desperately he wanted to fly, Charlie's broken wing kept him grounded at my place year round. Before he acquired Madame, he was desperate for a female who would stay with him. His piteous outbursts were constant reminders of the hardships that a flightless goose must endure.

The honking continued. "Oh, Charlie, you silly goose, what's bothering you now?" I asked. Charlie often stood under my bedroom window and clamored for me to feed him if I slept unusually late, but I had already fed him, so it wasn't me he wanted. This time his trumpeting was more persistent than ever.

Putting down my cup of coffee and setting aside the newspaper, I went into my bedroom in order to have the best vantage point. There was Charlie standing just below my window. Every honk was punctuated with a searching look around the pond. Then I noticed Madame, who echoed his outcries and scanned the pond as well. That's when I realized that Charlie Junior was missing. By golly, the little one had absconded and apparently without parental permission!

"I wonder where he is," I murmured as my eyes combed the area right along with them. I'd have honked too if I'd thought it would do any good.

As it turned out, the distraught parents didn't need my honking. Before long, little Charlie slowly slipped out of the tall grass around the pond and crept guiltily toward his elders. You could tell he knew he was in for it. His head practically between his webbed feet, he slunk toward his daddy, who immediately gave him heck. Big Charlie's head bobbed in Junior's face as he threatened his son within an inch of his life and nipped his neck relentlessly. But what happened next made me rub my eyes in disbelief. Charlie Junior did the same thing right back to his old man, including the neck nipping! They kept it up for quite a while, first Charlie fussing and then Junior sassing in reply. Suddenly they stopped and then began grazing as if nothing had happened. Junior must have learned his lesson because as far as I know, he didn't wander off again.

I couldn't help but think of my years in education. A youngster who showed that kind of insolence to his teacher would have been suspended for five to ten days and returned with a grudge as big as New York City. Perhaps geese are *not* so silly after all.

Bullies

What's the best way to handle a bully? Stand up to him? Ignore him? Fight if necessary? Back down if you know you're over-matched? Should parents ever be involved?

Canada geese are born bullies. They spend half their lives proving that they're the "baddest" critters around. Their weapons of choice are their bills. Don't let those cozy Christmas card drawings fool you. If a Canada goose is your enemy, a bulletproof vest and battle shield won't provide enough protection.

When Charlie first arrived at our pond, his broken wing made him the obvious target of the most cantankerous bullies. Still, he refused to surrender no matter how many times he was pecked with savage ferocity. Tony the Terrible, the Simon Legree of Kruger Pond's geese, was the ultimate bully. Diving at Charlie with a 100-yard running start, Tony would blast him with the impact of an assault rifle's ammunition. In spite of this punishment, Charlie kept hanging around and eating the food I provided. He even had the gall to go after Tony's mate, Carmella. Clearly he enjoyed living on the edge.

Persistence and bravado definitely pay off in the winged world. When Tony failed to return to our pond during the spring of 2006, Charlie began to attack unwanted marauders nearly as viciously as Tony had earlier assaulted him. Before long it was understood that Charlie had replaced Tony as head honcho of Kruger Pond.

During the first months of Charlie Junior's life, he was a mama's boy, hardly venturing out from under his mother's wing. Before his pinfeathers grew in, he ate, swam, and slept within inches of his mom. By the fall of 2007, he was only a few months old, but he had begun to look and act more like an adult.

He sported adult feathers, his feet were much larger, his legs had grown almost as long as his dad's, and his squeaky gosling voice began to make high-pitched honks. At this point he hung out with Charlie and began to copy his father's neck nipping, thrusting his neck forward the way Charlie did when he attacked another goose. I was certain that Junior had inherited Charlie's backbone and spunk as well. Charlie's offspring, I predicted, would be an even more formidable character due to his ability to fly. I couldn't have been more wrong!

In the fall of 2007, two families of geese stayed at Kruger Pond. One was Charlie's family—Charlie, Madame, and Charlie Junior, whom I fed on a daily basis. The other family knew that if they stayed with Charlie's group, there would be some corn left over for them. Although Charlie made a show of fighting them off, they patiently waited for him to eat his fill and then devoured what was left. This became established protocol.

On a cool November day, when I scattered corn in the usual feeding spot, Madame and Charlie attacked their fare with their usual gusto. However, the adult male from the second family chased Little Charlie away and ate his corn in full view of Big Charlie. I was sure that this bully was history. But Little Charlie surrendered his meal and slunk away without so much as a flapped feather.

I waited for Charlie Senior to deliver a death blow, but he did absolutely nothing. He completely ignored the fact that his son was being bullied by a larger goose and was too spineless to fight back. It seemed to me that Charlie Junior was a wimp and his daddy could not care less.

Perhaps this was Charlie Senior's way of teaching Junior to fight his own battles in order to survive in the wild. Charlie's philosophy was not to meddle. Period.

Potty Training

"It's time you and your family were potty trained!" I was exasperated with Charlie, Madame, and Charlie Junior. At first I was so elated that Charlie could attract a mate and sire a son that I overlooked the fact that I had to dodge their droppings in the driveway. The red snow shovel I used to clean it was in use year round.

"You know, Charlie, if you're smart enough to survive in your condition and charm Madame into giving up flying for you, you can darn well use the grass for your business and train your wife and son to do the same."

And so the lessons began. I methodically fetched the red snow shovel every morning, chased my recalcitrant geese out of the driveway, and proceeded to scoop up the mess as they watched every move I made. Satisfied that they understood my intention, I fed them corn in the grassy area a good distance away. The next day they were in the driveway again. My lessons had had no impact.

But I'm a teacher with enough experience to know that it takes some students longer than others to learn. "Okay, folks, I know you're smart. You can do this," I insisted.

Doggedly I continued to scrape the asphalt each day as they watched. Standing first on one foot and then the other, they drooled in anticipation and honked impatiently. "You'll get your corn once you learn that the driveway isn't your private bathroom. Other people have to use it too for far more diverse reasons," I lectured in my no-nonsense teacher voice.

Four days passed without evidence that my charges had reformed, and I had doubts about my feathered flock's capabilities. The break-through came on the fifth day—no droppings or geese sitting in the driveway!

Even Madame, who never abandoned her habit of hissing at me disapprovingly, stayed out of the driveway except for the extreme right corner. I decided to compromise with her and allow this aberration since scraping one corner of the driveway was easier than cleaning the entire asphalt surface.

In mid-winter I planned a cruise to the Panama Canal and asked my neighbor Leon to feed the geese while I was gone. Unfortunately I didn't share the toilet-training regimen with him, and when I returned, the driveway was a sea of pollution. The red shovel came out of retirement.

Charlie eventually became my assistant, and the other geese improved their hygiene as well. If I chased a renegade goose out of the driveway, Charlie took up the cause and gave the scoundrel a nasty nip. He was an unforgiving taskmaster and drove forgetful geese from forbidden territory even when I was inside.

The red shovel currently rests in the tool shed, and my company rarely hears "watch your step."

The Miracle

Some people may not believe that what happened is a miracle. I disagree. It all began with a phone call that I received just before Christmas in 2008. "Is—Is this Geraldine Kruger?" a man's voice asked.

"Yes," I answered.

"Do you have Canada geese on your pond that you write about?" he asked.

"Yes, I do." I had to smile. I have several friends who tell me they enjoy listening to the essays that I read on a National Public Radio station about Charlie, but this was the first time a stranger had called about them.

Charlie had been at my place since the year 2000. After eight years, he still didn't completely trust me. I can remember his eating out of my hand only once or twice and then with great hesitation. Charlie's distrustful and fearful nature led me to imagine that his broken wing and subsequent inability to fly were related to some extraordinary ordeal that had occurred between Canada and Virginia. Being a Canadian would explain why he didn't fit in with the Albemarle natives that predominate in this area. Sometimes I would look at Charlie and ask, "What happened to you, boy? I wish you could tell me your story."

"My name is Victor Lee," the telephone voice continued, "and I used to live on Tilman Road. I had a pond with some ducks, but in 1994 a nest of Canada geese hatched, and one of the goslings had a deformed wing and couldn't fly. I named him Gus and fed him, but he would never let me get too close to him.

"When my wife died and I remarried, I moved to Waynesboro and set up a pain clinic. In 2000, I sold my farm and left Gus behind because he was too wild to catch. I asked the new owners to feed him. Later they admitted that they hadn't fed him and he was no longer around. I've always wondered what happened to him."

"Did his broken wing stick straight out?" I asked, hardly believing what I was hearing. Tilman Road is less than a mile from where I live.

"Yes, and he would pick the feathers off." That clinched it. Charlie always picked the feathers from his broken wing as soon as new ones grew in every spring.

"I'm not sure whether his wing was broken when he was very young, or if he had a birth defect. I didn't notice that anything was wrong with him until his pinfeathers grew in."

Now my eight-year-old mystery was solved. I now knew that Charlie was a 14-year-old Albemarle native and that his disability originated from either a birth defect or a traumatic event that occurred when he was very young. Victor was amazed that Charlie was still around and happy that he'd found a good home. He was especially pleased to learn that Charlie had acquired a mate and sired a son.

A few days later Victor and his wife Nancy visited Charlie and verified that he was the same goose that hatched on their farm. Victor seemed disappointed that Charlie didn't appear to recognize him or react to being called "Gus." He also presented me with a wooden replica of a Canada goose that he had bought several years ago because it reminded him of his formerly adopted goose. He had written "Gus" on the bottom of it. It will permanently rest on the center of my dining room table.

Many normal geese don't survive disease and predators for 14 years, but Charlie's survival and acquisition of two caretakers who met through WVTF's essays made me wonder if this was more than a twist of fate.

Love On The Rocks

$\mathcal{M}$arriages on the rocks are commonplace in our society today. Not so in the world of Canada geese, who mate for life. At least that's what I used to think. Although Charlie's inability to fly made finding a mate next to impossible for him, he had captured the heart of Madame, who had presented him with Charlie Junior.

Almost a year after Charlie Junior's debut, I watched Madame clean out the reeds at the edge of the pond. Hardly taking time to rest, she gathered grass, twigs, and weeds until her nest was ready. Soon there were seven eggs, and Charlie swaggered and strutted like the star of a rock concert.

Still, I was wary of Madame's choice of venue. It provided no cover and, sure enough, one by one the eggs disappeared. When only one of the seven eggs remained, I stayed awake all night with the outside lights on, windows open, and two canoe paddles at the front door. Looking out of the window each time I heard the slightest sound, I never saw or heard any intruders, but the next morning the nest was empty.

After that, things were not the same between Charlie and Madame. Instead of grazing side by side, they stayed on opposite sides of the driveway. Little Charlie appeared to spend more time at his mother's side than Charlie did. With no goslings to rear, the distraught pair drifted aimlessly through lazy summer days and drifted apart as well.

Meanwhile Charlie Junior refused to leave Kruger Pond, and I could tell he was getting on Big Charlie's nerves. Big Charlie even chased Junior away if he inched close to the corn I scattered.

By the end of the summer, molting season was over. The Kruger Pond geese sported shiny new feathers and flew away. During the previous years, Madame had stayed with Charlie when the other geese left, but when it was clear that Junior wasn't going to leave with the rest of the flock that summered on Kruger Pond, Madame and Junior flew off together.

Lonely and bitterly depressed, Big Charlie paced back and forth, honking at the empty sky. "She's coming back, Charlie," I'd say. "She's just teaching Charlie Junior the ropes." I sang to him, even read him the newspaper, gratified that he would come close and listen to every word.

After two days, I awakened to thunderous honking. Sure enough, Madame had returned and without Charlie Junior. When the couple met, there was no disapproving neck nipping or head bobbing, and they appeared to resume their original relationship. Then Charlie Junior returned and mother and son left again, this time staying longer than before. Their coming and going became a pattern. Clearly Madame and Charlie were going through a trial separation. Perhaps with geese as well as humans, "happily ever after" exists only in fairy tales.

Missing Charlie

Charlie's life would have been idyllic if he had been the one to teach Charlie Junior to fly. When Madame and Little Charlie left him for occasional flying expeditions, Big Charlie was lonely and cold and honked incessantly.

It was on a chilly January afternoon in 2009 that I noticed a grayish-brown lump at the edge of the pond. I rushed to the creature, praying that it wasn't Charlie. Charlie had been a full-time member of my family for almost nine years. He'd been there for me during rough times, and I'd been his chief protector against ill-tempered dogs and other Canada geese. I'd watched him grow from a fainthearted six-year-old at the bottom of the pecking order to a nearly 15-year-old gander with more pluck and spunk than a triple-option quarterback.

The goose at the edge of the water was lying in a peculiar position and slowly lifted its head. I saw Charlie's deformed wing and winced. My eyes instinctively searched in vain for Little Charlie and Madame. They had left him again. When I touched him, his feathers felt icy and wet. He tried to turn over but couldn't.

Within seconds I was inside, calling the Wildlife Center, but there was no answer. I headed back to the pond, carrying a large red beach towel from my linen closet. I knelt beside Charlie, wrapping him in the towel and scooping him into my arms.

As soon as I took a step toward the house, he began to squirm. I set him down like a piece of fragile china. He stood up on his own and limped away from me as fast as he could toward the frozen pond. Then he hobbled across the ice to the woods.

The next morning there was no sign of Charlie, but Madame and Junior returned, continually craning their necks in search of him. Later I heard Charlie Junior's high-pitched honks. I followed his gaze and spied his dad, limping across the ice. Junior and Madame set out walking across the frozen pond to meet him, and I anticipated the climactic moment when they would reach each other. But Charlie stopped within 15 feet of them, did an about-face, and headed in the opposite direction. Was he playing hard to get?

You show 'em, Charlie, I thought. Undaunted, his mate and son reached him and remained by his side throughout the day.

But the next morning Junior and Madame were gone again. Charlie showed up to eat corn in his usual spot as if nothing out of the ordinary had happened.

"Are you all right, Charlie?" I bent down close to him and he didn't back away.

"Once Little Charlie learns how to live on his own, you and Madame can be together just like old times." I did my best to comfort him, and he seemed to understand.

But the next day, Charlie didn't come to his feeding spot. My neighbors and I searched every inch of our properties and found no trace of him or foul play. He's never come back.

I kept the feather that fell from the red beach towel beside Charlie's picture in my living room. Little Charlie and Madame visited me every day, but we all pined for Big Charlie's return. More than anything Charlie wanted to soar high above the treetops. Perhaps he's done just that.

My Charlie Boy

When Charlie first brought his raggedy-winged wreck of a body to our place, I had never seen a more pitiful goose. He longed to sample the tempting corn I threw out, but the pecking and stabbing he suffered from the bills of the other geese kept him from eating it. Charlie needed a friend, and for a while I was the only friend he had.

No matter how strong or vicious his opponents were, Charlie never shied away. He bounced back from punishment like a bruised and bloodied boxer refusing to go down. Mustering every ounce of strength, he warded off much more powerful geese that were capable of demolishing him. His determination, perseverance, and spirit made up for his lack of force and momentum. This lame, flightless goose ultimately became the champion of Kruger Pond.

Chief among Charlie's declarations of trust was his returning to me after I had committed the unpardonable sin of picking him up and carrying him in my arms. When he had nearly frozen to death, I cuddled him until he struggled to be free. After I set him on the ground, he refused to return no matter how loudly I cried, "Charlie Boy! Here, Charlie Boy!" But the next day it seemed all was forgiven. He allowed me near him as though nothing had happened. Without Junior and Madame around, I thought he would once again be my Charlie Boy, but I was mistaken. He left the next day and I never saw him again.

Since his disappearance, I have received a few reports of Charlie sightings. On a golf course in Crozet, a small town in Albemarle County not far from Kruger Pond, Nancy and Victor Lee spotted a Canada goose with a wing that stuck out to one side. They took pictures and e-mailed them to me. The deformed wing was on the left side just like Charlie's.

The following week Nancy, Victor, and I found the goose at the tenth hole of the golf club. I carried some corn in the plastic UVa cup that I had always used to feed Charlie. I held up the cup, shook it, and called, "Charlie Boy!" I even sang the song I used to sing to him: "Brown geese that fly with the moon on their wings / These are a few of my favorite things." Unimpressed, the goose slid into the water with the other geese and swam away.

On several other occasions, I returned to the golf course alone, but the alleged Charlie never came close to me. Once I found him grazing with a group of other geese on an open field. I rushed from my car toward them, throwing corn in my path. The other geese continued to graze, but the object of my visit took off running from me, slipped into the pond, and swam as far away from me as he could. Before he ran away, I caught a good look at his wing. It was straggly and hung down. Several feathers were dangling from it, almost touching the ground. Charlie always chewed the feathers off his deformed wing. All that was left of it was a stub that stuck straight out. Nothing indicated to me that this goose was my Charlie.

Thanks to my radio essays, Charlie has become a legend in Albemarle County and the surrounding area. I received an e-mail reporting another possible Charlie sighting shortly after his disappearance, but I've yet to be convinced that he is still alive. During a WVTF radio interview, I was asked if he could be replaced. How could you replace a goose that depended on you for food and water in winter? How could you replace a goose that needed your protection from his worst enemies? How could you replace a goose that trusted you more than he trusted any other human being? My Charlie Boy was an irreplaceable gift.

Charlie's Legacy

Charlie's disappearance has been difficult for me, but even more so for Charlie Junior and Madame. It wasn't until he left that I realized how much clout Charlie'd had. He was a fierce fighter and never backed down from the most malicious critters even though escaping his enemies was never guaranteed.

Charlie Junior was two years old when Big Charlie disappeared. Unfortunately it was already apparent that he hadn't inherited his old man's bravado. He'd cut and run whenever another goose plucked his feathers or made a threatening move. Geese have a way of taking on cylindrical shapes by elongating their necks as they attack other geese like feathered torpedoes. Frightened by this display, Junior and Madame ran away hungry rather than fight for the corn that I scattered.

In September 2009, I returned from a three-day trip to the beach to find Charlie's widow and son in the road near my mailbox. The other geese had driven them off my property, and they were afraid to set even one webbed foot in the yard. That did it! It was time Junior learned to stand up for himself.

Holding a canoe paddle high above my head, I chased the offending geese until they were forced to fly into the pond. If they attempted to swim to the other side, I ran and blocked their escape. Every time they tried to get out and graze, they came face to face with me.

Meanwhile, Madame and Little Charlie slowly made their way back home. I fed them tiny helpings of corn while fending off their tormentors with my paddle.

More than once, I crept behind some bushes and got down on my hands and knees, waiting for the marauders to come close. Just when they thought they had escaped me, I jumped up and emitted thunderous barks. Junior and Madame watched from the top of the hill, mightily impressed. I still wonder what the neighbors who happened by must have thought.

After several hours and countless mosquito bites, I thought I had convinced the interloping scoundrels that they were no longer welcome on Kruger Pond. In spite of this, they returned the next day. This time Charlie Junior and Madame stood beside me at the edge of the pond and helped me keep the bullies at bay. But when I left them to fend for themselves, Charlie Junior honked for my return if an interloper escaped the pond.

After three days of watching my battlefield tactics, Little Charlie torpedoed a goose on his own and drove him all the way into the pond. Big Charlie would have been proud.

AVAILABLE ON CD
On Kruger Pond: CHARLIE'S STORY
$12.95

To order the CD version of *On Kruger Pond: CHARLIE'S STORY*,
visit www.createspace.com/1990776.

www.ingramcontent.com/pod-product-compliance
Lightning Source LLC
Chambersburg PA
CBHW081759280526
45789CB00008B/2916